A Personal Tour of
HULL-HOUSE

LAURA B. EDGE

LERNER PUBLICATIONS COMPANY • MINNEAPOLIS

Cover: *The Hull-House parlor contains furniture similar to the type found there in the days of Jane Addams (in photograph).*

Title page: *Hull-House quickly evolved from a mansion into a row of brick buildings used for living, dining, learning, and sharing with other immigrants and Americans.*

Many thanks to Peggy Glowacki at the Jane Addams Hull-House Museum; Mary Ann Bamberger at the University of Illinois at Chicago Library, Special Collections; Mr. Hugh Saye; and the staffs of the Scenic Woods Library in Houston, Texas, and the Kingwood Library in Kingwood, Texas.

Dedicated to Gerry, Jeremy, and Jonathan, for their constant support

Lerner Publications Company
A division of Lerner Publishing Group
241 First Avenue North
Minneapolis, MN 55401 U.S.A.

Website address: www.lernerbooks.com

LIBRARY OF CONGRESS CATALOGING-IN-PUBLICATION DATA

Edge, Laura B.
  A personal tour of Hull-House / Laura B. Edge
    p.   cm. — (How it was)
    Includes bibliographical references and index.
    ISBN 0-8225-3582-3 (lib. bdg. : alk. paper)
    1. Hull House (Chicago, Ill.)—Juvenile literature. [1. Hull House (Chicago, Ill.)]
  I. Title. II. How it was (Minneapolis, Minn.)
  HV4196.C4 E33 2001
  362.84'009773'11—dc21   00-009241

Manufactured in the United States of America
1 2 3 4 5 6 – JR – 06 05 04 03 02 01

Contents

Businessman Charles Hull built this mansion in Chicago in 1856. The house was surrounded by trees and open space.

A house stands on a busy street,
Its doors are opened wide.

—from the Hull-House Women's
Club Anthem by Jane Addams

Introduction

Hull-House was one of the first settlement houses in the United States. Settlement houses were large community centers in poor areas of crowded cities. They were called settlement houses because the people who lived in them had chosen to settle among the poor. Often wealthy and well educated, settlement house workers wanted to improve life in slum neighborhoods.

The story of Hull-House began in 1856 when wealthy businessman Charles Hull built an elegant home in Chicago, Illinois. Surrounded by lawn and trees, it stood in a wealthy neighborhood on the edge of town. Hull and his family lived in the mansion for more than ten years.

Then Hull's wife and son died. He began traveling a great deal in connection with his real estate business. He rented the house to the Little Sisters of the Poor, a Catholic convent.

In October 1871, the Great Chicago Fire destroyed buildings throughout five square miles of the city.

The city gradually grew up around Hull's house. No longer on the outskirts of Chicago, it became part of a congested area known as the Nineteenth Ward.

In 1871 the Great Chicago Fire swept through the city, destroying most of the houses and other buildings in the Nineteenth Ward. "Hull's House," as neighbors called it, was one of the few houses to survive.

At that time, many newcomers were pouring into Chicago. Mostly immigrants from Europe, the new residents often could not afford good-quality homes. As Chicago scrambled to rebuild after the fire, builders in the Nineteenth Ward quickly erected the cheap housing these new residents needed. Many of the new homes were flimsy shacks and tenements—buildings where families were crowded into tiny apartments.

Most of the immigrants who moved into the Nineteenth Ward had never lived in a big city before. They couldn't speak English (although their children learned the language quickly). They didn't always understand American customs. They worked in low-paying factory jobs, barely earning enough money to feed their families. Sometimes several families moved into houses or apartments meant for one family. Conditions in the Nineteenth

In the late 1800s, parts of Chicago were in ruins. People crowded into shanties, or quickly built shacks, that provided minimal shelter and warmth.

Ward quickly deteriorated. Hull's house found itself in the middle of the worst slum in Chicago.

Day care was not available in that era. So mothers and fathers sometimes left their young children locked inside the tiny rooms of their tenement apartments until they got home from work. To help the family earn money, children often went to work at a young age. Many worked twelve or more hours a day by the time they were fourteen years old. They did not go to school.

Jane Addams was an educated and well-to-do young woman who had grown up in Illinois. She wanted to make the world a better place and to help others. She also wanted to find a useful purpose for her college education.

Together with her friend Ellen Gates Starr, Jane took a trip to Europe in the winter and spring of 1887 to 1888. In London, England, they discovered Toynbee Hall, the first settlement house in the world. A group of wealthy young men were working and living there in the middle of a London slum. Jane decided she wanted to follow their example.

In January 1889, Jane and Ellen moved to Chicago. They had no definite plan, but they knew they wanted to live as neighbors in a poor community. The minute they saw Hull's house, they realized they had found the perfect home. It looked run-down and odd, stuck between an

It is first in violence, deepest in dirt; loud, lawless, unlovely, ill-smelling, new; an overgrown gawk of a village, the 'tough' among cities, a spectacle for the nation.
—Chicago journalist Lincoln Steffens, describing Chicago in the early 1900s

undertaker's building and a saloon. But they could see that the two-story house had once been a fine home.

The house belonged to Helen Culver, a cousin of Charles Hull's who had inherited it after Hull's death. She rented the second floor of the house to Jane and Ellen. They moved in, together with Mary Keyser, their housekeeper, on September 18, 1889. But Helen Culver wanted to do more to support their efforts. She quickly decided to give Jane and Ellen a free lease on the entire house.

The women scrubbed, painted, and ordered repairs. They filled the rooms with family furniture and new mahogany furniture that matched the style of the house. Using Jane's savings, they bought a piano and some Oriental rugs. The mansion soon looked like a stately home again. High ceilings and ropelike carvings around the tall doors and windows gave it a welcoming look.

Since people called the place Hull's house, Jane and Ellen decided to name it Hull-House. They wanted Hull-House to become a place where people could relax, see fine art, and hear music. They hung paintings that they had bought in Europe. They invited musicians to entertain at evening gatherings.

And they began talking about their house to anyone who would listen. In the neighborhood, they walked around and shopped the outdoor markets to meet people. To get publicity, they attended teas, spoke at women's club meetings, and met with church groups. Newspaper reporters wrote stories about them.

As word spread, their neighbors began flocking to the house. Other wealthy young women who shared Jane Addams's ideas came to help. Some volunteered for an

The Continental United States

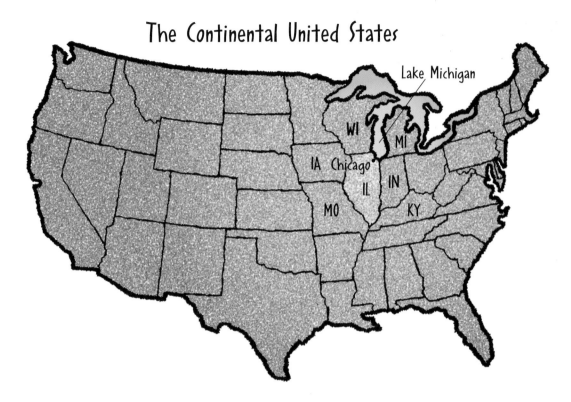

hour or two each day. Others began living at Hull-House. They all pitched in to bathe newborn babies, care for sick people, and watch children. They started a kindergarten, clubs, and classes.

In no time, Hull-House was bursting at the seams. Fifty thousand visitors passed through Hull-House during the first year alone. The clatter of Irish dancing and the aroma of Italian cooking filled the air. Adults studied English while young people read Shakespeare, took art classes, or learned to play musical instruments.

Hull-House was so successful that it quickly ran out of space. Jane and Ellen began looking for ways to expand.

The Hull-House complex included the Hull Mansion itself, which was remodeled in 1895 to include a third story. Other additions included the Butler Art Gallery (1891); the Music School (1893); a children's building, sometimes called the Smith Building (1895); the Jane Club, a co-operative boardinghouse for working women (1898); and the Coffee-house and Theater (1899). The 1900s saw the addition of the Labor Museum and Gymnasium (1900); the Men's Club Building, which housed the Juvenile Protective Association on the first floor (1902); the Hull-House Apartments (1902); Bowen Hall, often called the Women's Club Building (1904); the Residents' Dining Hall (1905); the Boys' Club Building (1906); and the Mary Crane Building (1907).

Helen Culver donated land around the house, and Jane and Ellen hired two architects, Irving and Allen Pond. With money given by wealthy patrons, they added a new building, then another and another. Between 1891 and 1907, Hull-House became a complex of thirteen buildings sprawled over a full city block!

Living in the middle of the misery of the Nineteenth Ward, the women who lived and worked at Hull-House became involved in improving the neighborhood. They worked night and day to clean up filthy streets. They investigated illnesses caused by poor living and working conditions. They helped to pass laws to protect the safety and health of children. Jane Addams and other Hull-House residents, such as Julia Lathrop, Florence Kelley, and Alice Hamilton, became nationally known.

Come along as we spend a day at Hull-House. It is winter in the windy city of Chicago. The year is 1908, and dawn is breaking. . . .

A long, curving staircase covered by a red carpet leads to the entryway of Hull-House.

It was obvious that if you went to the House you were welcome; if you called, you were called upon; and if you let the young women know there was anything they could do for you, they did it if they could.

—James Linn, Jane Addams's nephew

With Jane Addams

Jane Addams opened her eyes and stretched as morning light danced through the narrow window of her bedroom. She looked at her favorite oil painting hanging on the wall opposite her bed and thought about the day ahead. Eager to begin, she got out of bed, walked briskly to her wooden bureau, and began to dress.

Jane finished buttoning her high-necked collar, then turned and walked to the window that overlooked Halsted Street. Horse-drawn carriages rattled clumsily down the muddy street. Not a single blade of grass could be seen in the dirty, smelly neighborhood. Wooden houses, originally built for one family and more recently occupied by several, were falling down. Garbage overflowed from wooden boxes fastened to the street pavement. Small children, skinny, pale, and dressed in rags, were running around as people hurried to work or to the market.

We have so much to do, Jane Addams thought. The sound of knocking at the front door drew her away from the window and quickly out her bedroom door. She hurried down the long, winding stairway to the first floor, her floor-length green silk dress rustling as she passed into the entryway. She opened the front door. On the broad porch stood a young Italian mother with a baby in her arms. A three-year-old girl clutched her mother's skirt.

With tears in her eyes, the young woman explained her problem in Italian. A friend took care of her children while she worked each day, but the friend was sick.

Though busy with running Hull-House, Jane Addams (in white shirt) *took time to greet visitors at the door and direct them to various parts of the house.*

Hull-House

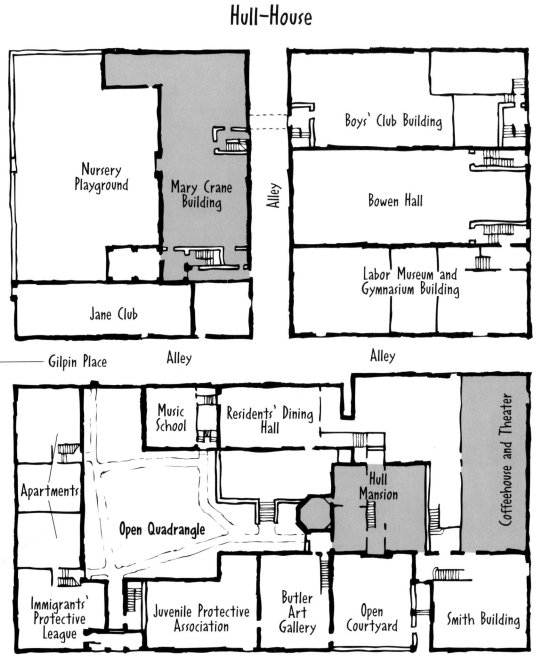

Boys' Club Building

Bowen Hall

Labor Museum and Gymnasium Building

Nursery Playground

Mary Crane Building

Alley

Jane Club

Gilpin Place

Alley

Alley

Polk Street

Music School

Residents' Dining Hall

Coffeehouse and Theater

Apartments

Open Quadrangle

Hull Mansion

Immigrants' Protective League

Juvenile Protective Association

Butler Art Gallery

Open Courtyard

Smith Building

Halsted Street

Residents and guests enjoyed a hearty breakfast in the Coffeehouse.

The mother could not afford to miss a day of work or the family would have no food. Was it true that the women of Hull-House took care of children?

Jane was glad she had lived in Italy and could speak Italian. She smiled, took the baby, and told the mother she'd be glad to watch the children. Then Jane invited the woman to join her for breakfast. The woman shook her head no and kissed her children good-bye. With a mumbled word of thanks, she dashed down the street and disappeared into the city.

Holding the little girl's hand and carrying the baby, Jane took them down a covered walkway to the Coffeehouse. The mouth-watering smell of baking biscuits and breads reached them as they entered. After a breakfast of fresh oranges, milk, and warm biscuits with butter and jam, Jane led the children to their next stop.

The little group walked through the reception room of the Hull Mansion. The tiny girl holding Jane's hand stared wide-eyed around her. The room was so elegant, its furnishings much grander than any she had ever seen: a horsehair sofa, mahogany chairs, and a marble mantle. Jane pointed out the beautiful pictures on the walls, which she had bought when she had lived in Europe.

The threesome next scurried across the alley to the Mary Crane Building. Mr. R. T. Crane had donated it as a memorial to his wife, Mary. Inside, they climbed the stairs to the third floor.

Jane Addams decorated the reception room of Hull-House with her own favorite paintings. The mahogany chairs invited weary visitors to rest and chat.

They had arrived at the Hull-House crèche—a place for young children. The crèche included a nursery for infants, a playroom for toddlers, a nursery school classroom, a kindergarten classroom, and a playroom for school-aged children whose parents worked and didn't get home until late. It also offered child care classes for parents.

The Hull-House complex, made up of thirteen buildings, covered about five acres. Two alleys divided the complex into one large and two small groups. The buildings bordering Halsted Street were connected by halls, corridors, and stairs. People needed lots of practice to get from one place to another without getting lost!

A group of very young children was seated on the floor, their eyes fixed on their teacher. She was reading a story. Her eyes twinkled, and her voice seemed full of laughter as she created a make-believe world.

The little girl with Jane plopped happily down on the floor with the other children.

Jane stood at the back of the room, still holding the baby. She watched the class for a few minutes. Then she carried the baby up the stairs to the fourth floor. A teacher there spoke quietly with Jane for a few minutes. Jane gently settled the baby into a cozy white crib.

From the Mary Crane Building, Jane walked back to the Hull Mansion and headed for the octagon, an eight-sided room in the center of the house. On the dark paneling that covered its walls from floor to ceiling, Jane had hung pictures she loved and photographs of her father and her friends. In the center of the room stood her desk, a gift from her sisters.

Hull-House resident Alice Hamilton opened a well-baby clinic in the basement of the Mary Crane Building. Volunteers bathed young children there and offered health hints to mothers. The Hull-House visiting nurse program sent trained nurses into the neighborhood to visit new mothers and help them learn new and better ways to care for their youngsters.

Jane sat down and began opening her huge stack of mail. In the nineteen years since she had moved in, interest in Hull-House had spread across the nation. Many of the letters were from people who wanted to hear about the house and its programs.

Jane also had a speech to prepare. She traveled often to tell people about the work at Hull-House. She also spoke about rights for women, children, and workers. And she had many stories to tell about the work of her friends Julia Lathrop and Alice Hamilton, who were living at Hull-House. Jane was constantly jotting down ideas on bits of paper that she saved. When she was ready to draft a speech, she chose the bits of paper she wanted to use.

As Jane began working on a speech, her friend Ellen Gates Starr appeared in the doorway. Like Jane, Ellen had been a resident of Hull-House for many years. Ellen had

Jane Addams had her office in the octagon room. In 1908 the room had dark paneling.

brought Mr. Andolini, an unemployed factory worker, with her. Ellen and Jane were trying to find a job for him. Jane gave Mr. Andolini the name of a nearby necktie factory that needed workers.

Then Jane walked Mr. Andolini to the front door. On their way, they passed a group of women in the parlor. The women were discussing a strike at the shoe factory. They were afraid that the strike (refusal to work) would put them out of work.

Residents lived all over the Hull-House complex. Single women lived in bedrooms on the second and third floors of the Hull Mansion or in the Mary Crane Building. Single men lived in the Butler Building. Married couples lived in apartments facing Ewing Street and the Boys' Club Building.

Mrs. Kiel, an immigrant from Germany, timidly entered the house as Jane said good-bye to Mr. Andolini. When Jane said hello, it was clear that Mrs. Kiel couldn't speak English. In German, Jane told her, "I'm pleased to meet you." Mrs. Kiel smiled broadly when Jane invited her to join an evening English class at Hull-House.

Urgent banging on the front door interrupted their conversation. When Jane opened the door, a tiny woman with a black babushka (scarf) over her head stepped inside. She hurriedly explained that a policeman had taken her seven-year-old son away. The boy had stolen some coal from a railway freight car because his grandmother was cold and the train seemed to have plenty. The woman didn't know where her son had been taken. She frantically asked Jane for help.

Jane grabbed her coat and led the woman to the police station. The woman's son was there. Jane talked to a judge, and he released the boy. Jane smiled as mother and child were reunited.

Walking back to Hull-House, Jane could see that the children in the neighborhood were running home from school. She waved at Eleni, a small Greek girl, as Eleni raced by and headed for her afternoon classes at Hull-House.

In the Hull-House library, adults could read magazines and newspapers in English and in foreign languages.

May you find hope who enter here.
—motto hanging over the entrance to Hull-House

With Eleni

Eleni skipped through the door of the Butler Building and into her favorite place in the whole world—the Hull-House reading room. The reading room was part of a larger adult library, a branch of the Chicago Public Library. Warm and inviting, the reading room contained a wonderful selection of children's books as well as a collection of toys from around the world. Eleni agreed with the plaque on the wall: "Happy is the child with books." She often spent hours reading in this room, lost in imaginary worlds where children were never cold and always had enough to eat.

Eleni hurriedly returned her book, checked out another, and raced across the courtyard to the Smith Building. She ran up the stairs to the art studio, which occupied the entire top floor. She couldn't wait to get started! Students in art class had been asked to create something that reminded them of their homeland.

Hull-House

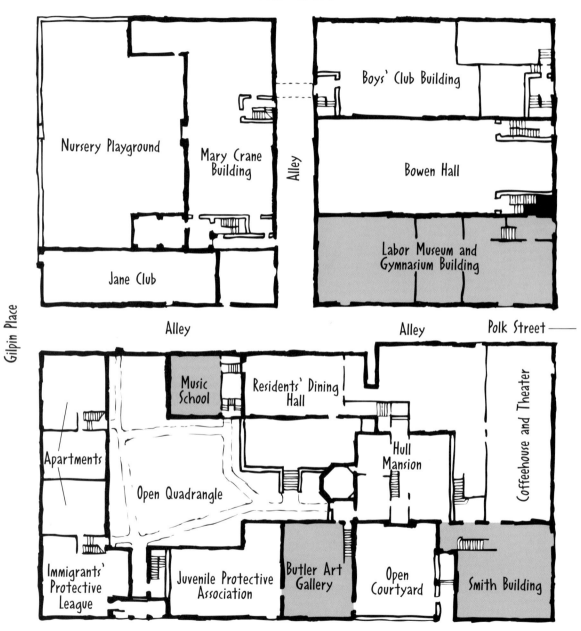

They could use paint, crayons, chalk, or clay. Eleni planned to build a model of the Parthenon, an ancient temple in her beloved Athens, Greece.

Eleni waved to her friend Carmella and hurried to a table at the back of the room. She hummed a little tune as she slapped a lump of wet clay on the table and began to mold it. As Eleni transformed the blob of clay, a smile slipped across her face, and memories of her homeland washed over her. She patted her structure and added finishing touches. There! A beautiful building from home had arrived at Hull-House.

After Eleni finished her masterpiece, she wandered around the classroom, looking at her friends' work. Ivan had made the palace of Peter the Great in Russia. Carmella had created the dome of St. Peter's, a cathedral in Rome, Italy. Hans had painted a German castle with the snowcapped peaks of the Alps in the background.

Art classes included painting, drawing, clay modeling, lettering, and design.

The Hull-House complex included (right to left) *the Boys' Club, Bowen Hall, the Gymnasium, and the Coffeehouse and Theater.*

Eleni and her friends giggled excitedly as they talked about the trip they were taking to the Chicago Art Institute next week. Miss Starr had shown them photographs of Renaissance paintings hanging at the institute, and on Saturday she was taking them there to see the real-life paintings.

Before Eleni knew it, the next class began streaming into the studio. She hurried down the stairs and out the door, then walked down Polk Street and cut across to the alley entrance to the Gymnasium Building. She walked through the textile room and into the cooking room. It was empty. Eleni's stomach grumbled as she remembered yesterday's cooking lesson. She wished she had another cooking class and another serving of warm bread oozing with butter.

Eleni skipped on to the dressmaking room behind the cooking room. Her sewing class met here once a week. Eleni was making a dress from a blue cotton fabric dotted with dainty pink flowers. Eleni's teacher greeted her and the other students and gently reminded them to be careful and take their time. Eleni frowned as she tried to make each stitch the same size. She didn't want to take her time. She wanted to finish the dress, the finest she'd ever owned, and wear it.

Finally the dress looked done. Eleni jumped out of her chair and flew across the room to her teacher. She crossed her fingers behind her back, hopped from one foot to the other, and chewed on her bottom lip as her teacher examined the garment. She couldn't stifle a whoop of delight when her teacher pronounced the dress "finished."

Carefully holding her new dress, Eleni left the Gymnasium Building, crossed the alley, walked through the Coffeehouse, down the covered walkway, and through the Hull Mansion and Residents' Dining Hall to the Music School. Eleanor Smith, the founder and director of the Music School, had composed the violin music that Eleni would practice.

Miss Smith was also Eleni's teacher. The class was

Children waited in the Music School for lessons that would prepare them for recitals.

rehearsing for a concert that would be performed on Sunday afternoon in the Hull-House Residents' Dining Hall. Larger concerts, like the upcoming Christmas Concert and Tableaux, were held in Bowen Hall.

Eleni strolled to the violin stand. She had been taking lessons for a year. With each lesson, her love for the mellow, soothing sounds of her instrument grew stronger. She stroked her horsehair bow across the strings of the violin, and the group of boys and girls filled the room with music.

Eleni looked up in surprise when a new group of girls

and boys began filing into the room, talking in many different languages. Could an hour really be over so soon? She loosened the strings on her bow and carefully returned the violin to its stand.

Eleni's classes were over for the day. It was time to go home. She dragged her toes across the carpet as she walked slowly through the Hull Mansion and out the front door. Daydreaming about how nice she'd look in her new dress, Eleni walked head down as she made her way up Halsted Street. No wonder she plowed into Tony, whose face was covered with grime from the factory he'd worked in all day. Eleni couldn't help but laugh when Tony twirled around, tipped his hat, and raced off down the street toward the Boys' Club Building.

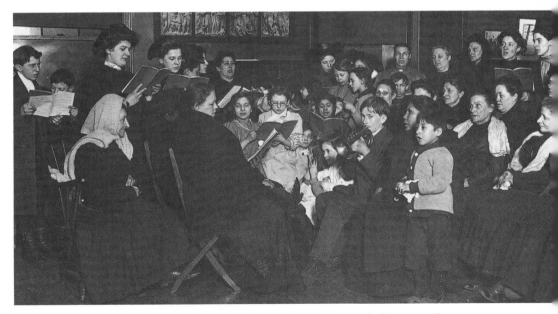

Singing classes at Hull-House brought together people of all ages. This photograph shows a class from 1910.

The Boys' Club library was a pleasant place for boys of all ages to spend time.

With Tony

Tony ricocheted through the door of the Boys' Club Building, a place devoted to boys under the age of sixteen. The large five-story building had classrooms, clubrooms, a game room, a billiard room, a bowling alley, a toy room, a band room, a library, a study, a wood shop, a tin shop, and a printing shop complete enough to publish a small newspaper.

Tony and his friends were all members of the Young Heroes Club. For weeks, Miss Mary Rozen Smith had been reading the story of the French king Charlemagne to them. She had come to the point of Count Roland's last battle. As Miss Smith began, Tony shoved Nico and Angelo pushed Frank. They were jostling for position near Miss Smith. She paused. In the blink of an eye, silence blanketed the room, and she continued.

The scene came alive in Tony's imagination. His heart

pounded as brave Count Roland wielded his mighty sword, Durendal. Tony saw the sun sparkle off glistening shields. He heard a thousand trumpets blasting. A chorus of cheers went up from the group as the valiant knights fought for their king. Tony cheered loudest of all.

Tony spent almost all of his free time at the Boys' Club Building. Listening to Miss Smith's stories was his favorite activity, but he could do lots of other things too, like play games.

In the Boys' Club game room, boys could play pool, checkers, table tennis, and lots of other games.

Hull–House

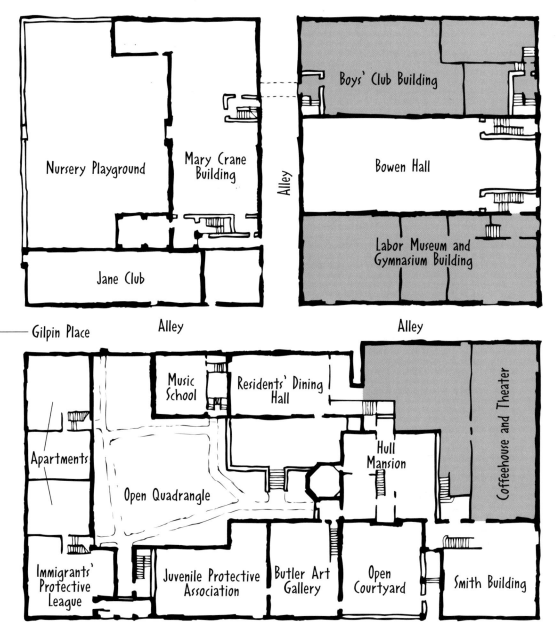

Nursery Playground

Mary Crane Building

Jane Club

Alley

Boys' Club Building

Bowen Hall

Labor Museum and Gymnasium Building

Gilpin Place

Alley

Alley

Polk Street

Music School

Residents' Dining Hall

Apartments

Open Quadrangle

Hull Mansion

Coffeehouse and Theater

Immigrants' Protective League

Juvenile Protective Association

Butler Art Gallery

Open Courtyard

Smith Building

Halsted Street

The boys in the wood shop made most of the games in the game room. They painted checkerboards on tabletops. They used bottle corks for checkers or made checkers by sawing broom handles into small disks.

The large game room also held two table tennis tables with table tennis paddles also made by the boys. Tony picked up one of the paddles and played a wild game with Angelo. Angelo won, but only by one point, and Tony challenged him to a rematch the next day. Then he trotted off to the Gymnasium Building.

In the Gymnasium Building, Tony ran up the stairs to the gymnasium on the third floor. He heard the unmistakable rat-a-tat-tat of the boxing team pounding away on punching bags. Tony grinned and flexed his muscles like a muscle man as he passed his friend Danny.

Tony belonged to a basketball team, the Tigers. They were practicing for the Cook County Basketball Tournament. Another Hull-House team, the Midgets, had won the tournament last year, and Tony wanted his team to win this year. Tony warmed up, dribbling down the court and tossing some practice shots. As he started horsing around with his teammates, he heard the shrill blast of his coach's whistle announcing his favorite part of practice. Scrimmage!

An hour later, sweaty and panting, Tony and his pals strutted out of the gym and down the stairs to the shower room on the second floor. Look out Cook County, Tony thought. The Tigers were ready!

Tony left the Gymnasium Building by the door to the alley and crossed to the Coffeehouse and Theater. Upstairs on second floor, Tony opened the theater's heavy door.

Live theater was very popular in the early 1900s. Workers at Hull-House understood that the children of the Nineteenth Ward needed the magic of theater. So they provided children with a theater of their own, complete with a pipe organ. Hull-House productions included plays by Shakespeare, Schiller, and Molière. Scores of children researched the historical periods of the plays to make sets and costumes copied from old pictures. They spent hours memorizing difficult lines and learning to pronounce the words correctly.

He stood for a moment in the entrance, savoring the magic of the place. A life-size mural of Abraham Lincoln pushing a flatboat down the Mississippi River covered one wall. The mural on the opposite wall showed the Russian writer and philosopher Leo Tolstoy plowing a field with a wooden hand plow. "Act well your part, there all the honor lies," read a sign above the stage.

Excited and nervous at the same time, Tony walked toward the stage. He was playing the role of Little John in the play *Robin Hood,* and dress rehearsal was about to begin. He made his way to a small changing room backstage. He buttoned his velvet doublet, adjusted his pointed shoes, and picked up his jeweled sword. Then he joined the other cast members as they gathered onstage. Tony's friend Hilda wore a blue satin dress with paste emeralds and pearls and a coral satin petticoat. A filmy veil fluttered from her peaked cap.

Edith de Nancrede, the director of the play, gave the cast some last-minute instructions. She encouraged the boys and girls to relax and have fun. Tony thought he could handle that, and he did, even though he forgot some of his lines and tripped on his pointy shoes. Tony was glad they had a few more chances to rehearse in their costumes before performing for an audience.

After rehearsal, Tony walked through the covered walkway to the Hull Mansion. The clatter of dishes and the jumble of voices drifted toward him from the dining room. His grumbling stomach reminded him that he hadn't eaten since breakfast. With a glance over his shoulder, he scurried out the door and raced home to his mother, four sisters, and dinner.

Hull-House residents and visitors ate in the Residents' Dining Hall (above), *which faced a courtyard.*

The Hull-House dining room had long, wooden tables that brought together people from many different countries.

Classes at Hull-House were never just classes
where people came to learn a specific subject. There
was a human element of friendliness among us.
—Hilda Satt Polacheck, a Polish immigrant and Hull-House guest

With Bridget

Inside the Hull-House dining room, Bridget shifted in her chair and smoothed her skirt. She looked around the paneled room with its huge fireplace and high-beamed ceiling. Light from the setting sun streamed through the large windows, reflecting off Spanish wrought-iron chandeliers. Seated at the head of the table was Jane Addams. Scattered throughout the room were famous authors, professors, and business leaders.

This was Bridget's first visit to Hull-House. Her friend Angelina came here all the time. When Miss Mary Hill, a resident Bridget had met at the market, invited her to come for dinner, Bridget's curiosity got the better of her. She decided to see for herself what Angelina found so interesting in the big house on the corner.

At dinner, Bridget nibbled her food. She listened intently to the conversation whizzing around her.

Hull-House

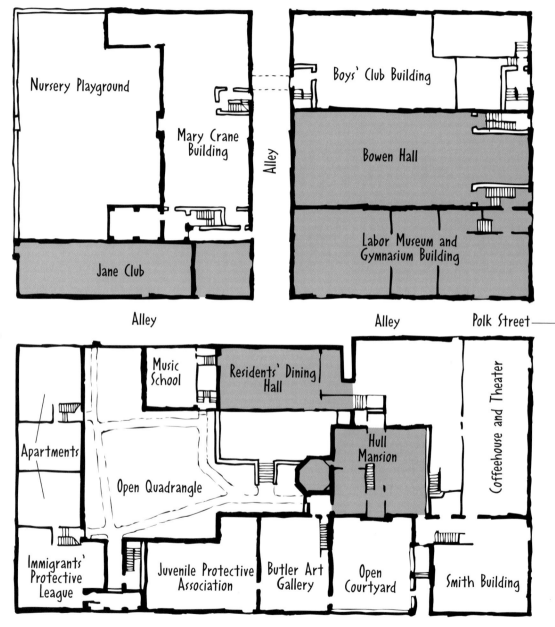

Nursery Playground

Mary Crane Building

Alley

Boys' Club Building

Bowen Hall

Labor Museum and Gymnasium Building

Jane Club

Gilpin Place

Alley

Alley

Polk Street

Music School

Residents' Dining Hall

Coffeehouse and Theater

Apartments

Open Quadrangle

Hull Mansion

Immigrants' Protective League

Juvenile Protective Association

Butler Art Gallery

Open Courtyard

Smith Building

Halsted Street

When the discussion turned to factories, Jane asked her to describe the knitting factory where she worked. Bridget put down her fork and took a deep breath as all eyes turned to her. Even though she was a grown woman, she felt timid and her mind went blank. Why would the famous people at this table want to hear her opinion? Bridget looked at the kind expression on Jane's face. People in the group were nodding encouragement. Suddenly Bridget felt the courage to begin.

Bridget described how she worked from seven in the morning until six in the evening, six days a week. She spent the half-hour lunch break in front of her knitting machine. She had started working when she was just fourteen years old, then earning four dollars a week. As an experienced worker, she earned six dollars a week. Laws regarding safety devices in the factory didn't exist, so accidents occurred frequently. Bridget said the workers might go on strike because of these conditions. If that happened, Bridget would not be able to pay her rent.

One woman at the table told Bridget that Hull-House might have a solution. Bridget could live at the Jane Club. The Jane Club had been started in 1891 in an apartment on Ewing Street. When the club needed more space, it was moved to a three-story house with twenty-four bedrooms. The house had a kitchen, dining room, drawing room, library, and laundry. The "Janes" each paid three dollars a week for dues. When a strike put one of the Janes out of work, the others paid her bills until the strike was over. Bridget couldn't believe her ears. If the workers did go on strike, she would still have a place to live!

After dinner, Miss Hill took Bridget's arm and led her

The idea for the Jane Club sprang from some women who worked at a shoe factory. They wanted to go on strike, which meant giving up their pay. If they went too long without pay, they wouldn't be able to pay their rent. One woman suggested that they all live together. That way, they could stand by each other when times were tough.

The Jane Club opened its doors in May 1891. It was the first club of its kind in the United States. Hull-House paid the first month's rent for the Jane Club house. After that, the members paid the rent. Each gave three dollars a week to cover house expenses.

to the Labor Museum in the Gymnasium Building. As they crossed the alley, Miss Hill explained that Jane had started the Labor Museum. Jane had noticed that American-born children often thought their immigrant parents were old-fashioned. The Labor Museum was meant to help bring these children and their parents from the Old World—Europe—closer together.

The Labor Museum was a combination workshop-

museum. People learned traditional crafts there. But anyone could visit to watch the craftspeople work. Visitors
learned the history of the craft and the Old World tradi-
tions. They could also browse through the museum's
displays and purchase goods that had been made there.

The first stop for Bridget and Miss Hill was the wood

At the Labor Museum, young people could see how clothing had
been made in earlier times through demonstrations. These displays of
spinning and weaving made the children proud of their parents' backgrounds and skills. Gradually the Labor Museum grew to include other
crafts such as woodworking and metalworking.

and metal shop. Bridget looked around in amazement. The room bustled with groups of workers at their tasks. Clanging copper, pounding hammers, and rasping saws followed Bridget and Miss Hill as they circled the room.

Most of the young men in the shop worked at boring factory jobs during the day. Working in the shop in the evenings taught them how to make useful things. These new skills gave the young men a sense of pride in good workmanship and a respect for things of beauty.

One group of young men was making sleds. Some of the men were cutting the wood, others were sanding it to a smooth finish, and still others were carving designs into

In the Labor Museum, immigrants taught children and adults handicrafts such as weaving and embroidery.

the wood. In another part of the room, the whirl of a potter's wheel had drawn a group of visitors. They watched as a man created a sleek bowl from a rough lump of clay. Behind him stood a case filled with pottery for sale to the public.

From the wood and metal shop, Bridget and Miss Hill walked through the dressmaking and cooking areas to the textile room. Bridget noticed several women dressed in native costumes of Greece, Italy, Russia, and Ireland. They were showing a group of visitors how hand spinning and hand weaving had been done in the Old World. Four display cases lined one wall. They overflowed with articles showing the evolution of techniques for making cotton, wool, silk, and linen.

Hull-House was the first settlement house in the United States to have both male and female residents. To become a resident, people had to apply. The first step was to live at the house for six weeks. Then the residents decided whether or not the new person had contributed well to the work of the house. If so, he or she could stay. If not, he or she was kindly asked to leave.

Bridget smiled as she studied the different machines for spinning, from stick spindles to several types of spinning wheels. Miss Hill asked Bridget if she'd like to try a spinning wheel. Bridget agreed and sat beside a plump, good-natured Russian woman coaxing linen thread from a bunch of flax on a spindle. The Russian woman showed her how to press a pedal with her foot to turn the wheel.

It was time to go, since this week's meeting of the Women's Club was about to begin. Bridget and Miss Hill

Bowen Hall (above) *housed the Women's Club, where women of all backgrounds met and talked about subjects such as child care and winning the right to vote.*

left the Labor Museum and walked next door to Bowen Hall. Women from many different countries belonged to the Women's Club. Some were highly educated, while others couldn't read or write. But every member was considered equal. They met weekly to discuss topics affecting women and the care of children.

Miss Hill told Bridget that she had been looking forward to this meeting for weeks. A national leader in the fight for women's suffrage—the right to vote—was scheduled to speak.

Bridget and Miss Hill slipped through the crowded room and found empty chairs. Just then the president of the club, Louise deKoven Bowen, called the meeting to order. Following parliamentary procedure, she led a discussion of one club project, the Alzina Stevens Linen

Chest. Poor people or those too sick to work could come to the Hull-House complex and receive clothing and supplies from the linen chest.

Next Mrs. Bowen introduced the speaker. Bridget craned her neck to see over the women seated in front of her. She soaked up every word as the speaker passionately described why women deserved the vote. After about forty-five minutes, Mrs. Bowen started a discussion. Opinions of all kinds came out in the lively debate that followed. Listeners were tolerant and accepting.

Bridget left Bowen Hall inspired. She walked back to the Hull Mansion, where her friend Angelina was in the dining room in a citizenship class. The people in the class were studying the U.S. Constitution. They were preparing for a test to become U.S. citizens. As Bridget waited for Angelina, she thought that the women in the class would not truly be citizens until they could vote.

Bridget and Angelina snuggled into their warm coats before stepping out into the cold night air. Angelina asked Bridget if she'd enjoyed her visit to Hull-House. Bridget bubbled with excitement as she talked about her evening. Angelina invited Bridget to come to a dance with her on Saturday night and watch her show off the waltz and two-step she'd learned in dancing class. Bridget laughed and said she wouldn't miss it.

The friends parted. Bridget hurried home, her hands stuffed in her pockets. She wanted to start reading the book Miss Hill had given her for a reading class tomorrow night. Frosty breath swirled around her face as she conjured up images from the evening, leaving cold and gritty Halsted Street far behind.

The children of the Nineteenth Ward entertained themselves by playing games outside.

Even in the very first years of Hull-House we began to discover that our activities were gradually extending from the settlement to a participation in city and national undertakings.

—Jane Addams

With Florence Kelley

Jane Addams looked out the window. Darkness blanketed the neighborhood, and she could barely see the trolleyline outside. Halsted Street was nothing but a long, coal-black tunnel dimly lit by street lamps. Most of the residents of Hull-House were settling in after a long day. Jane was expecting her friend Florence Kelley to arrive for a visit. Jane shivered as she thought of her dear friend traveling in the windy dark. In the quiet of this cold and blustery night, she could hear the old house creak and moan. A grandfather clock ticked in the hallway.

Then the front door opened, letting in a chilly blast off Lake Michigan. Florence Kelley stepped inside. Her brown hair glistened with wet snow. Jane ran into the entry hall to greet her. The two friends beamed as they said hello and Florence took off her winter coat.

The two women turned around as they heard footsteps on the stairs behind them. Two Hull-House residents—Julia Lathrop and Alice Hamilton—were hurrying downstairs. They had been listening for Florence, too. Florence hugged each woman in turn. These friends lived too far from her own home in New York! She missed the years when she had lived at Hull-House.

Chicago newspapers had called these women a "galaxy of stars." They had each helped to improve life for people in the neighborhood, in Illinois, and across the nation. And each was continuing that important work in her own way. They had so much to talk about!

Florence rested her hand on the dark railing of the stairs as she began telling her friends about her long train trip from New York. Then Ellen Gates Starr appeared. The reunion of friends was complete.

The five women stepped into the parlor. Florence looked around the familiar room. A fire burned brightly in the fireplace, and the room blazed with light. Its fine furnishings, brass ceiling light, and elegant wallpaper reminded Florence of how different home life was for most people in this neighborhood.

A copy of a book titled *Hull-House Maps and Papers* rested on a gleaming tabletop. It had been written by Jane Addams, Florence Kelley, and other residents of Hull-House. The book told about their study of the people who lived in a ten-block area around the house.

Hull-House Maps and Papers was the first detailed description of immigrant communities in an American city. The book helped bring about changes in social welfare.

Florence had written about

Those who lived at and visited Hull-House warmed their hands and feet by the parlor's fireplace.

the many neighborhood children who worked at home. They helped their parents sew on buttons, stitch hems, and add other handwork to garments made in Chicago's bustling factories. As Florence had seen, many of their homes were damp basement apartments, crowded and dirty. The work was so hard that these home businesses were called sweatshops. She was glad that so much had happened in the years since to help those children.

Florence looked into the gray eyes of her friend Jane to whom so many people owed so much!

Hull-House

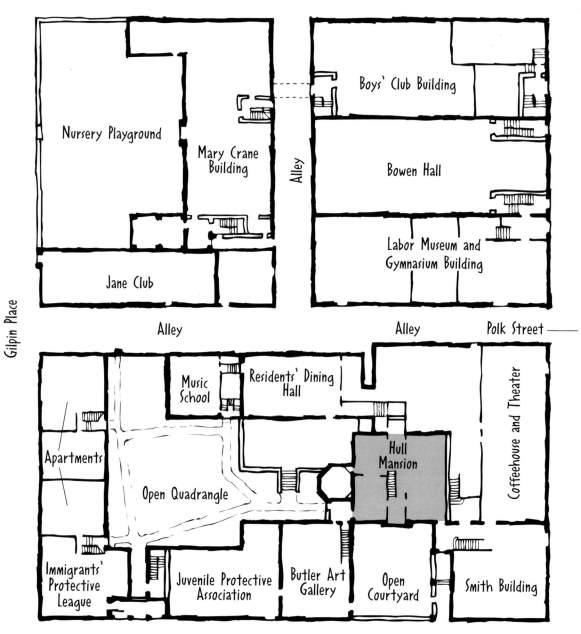

Gilpin Place

Nursery Playground

Mary Crane Building

Alley

Boys' Club Building

Bowen Hall

Labor Museum and Gymnasium Building

Jane Club

Alley

Alley

Polk Street

Music School

Residents' Dining Hall

Apartments

Open Quadrangle

Hull Mansion

Coffeehouse and Theater

Immigrants' Protective League

Juvenile Protective Association

Butler Art Gallery

Open Courtyard

Smith Building

Halsted Street

Just this evening on the train, Florence had met a young man who had once lived at Hull-House. He had said, "Without Jane Addams, Hull-House is nothing." Florence Kelley knew what he meant. All the residents of Hull-House pitched in. Yet it was Jane who kept everyone inspired. Many people called Hull-House simply "the place where Miss Addams lives."

The women clustered around the fireplace with its carved mantle. Julia Lathrop sat down on one of the

Jane Addams sometimes met in the reception room with friends such as Julia Lathrop, Ellen Gates Starr, Florence Kelley, and Dr. Alice Hamilton to discuss how they might change conditions in the city— and the world.

mahogany chairs. She reached down and loosened the ties on her leather shoes. Her feet were sore from all the walking she did on her job visiting Chicago orphanages, hospitals, poorhouses, and other public institutions. The Turkish carpet underfoot felt soft and warm.

Ellen passed a bowl of fruit. The women ate fruit, sipped tea, and shared their latest news with Florence. Alice explained her study of illnesses, such as lead poisoning, caused by poor working conditions. She spoke with keen intelligence. She didn't seem a bit tired!

Julia closed her eyes and let her thoughts drift. She thought about a skinny, solemn-faced, eight-year-old boy she had met that morning. He had stolen some milk for his baby sister. Tomorrow he would appear before a judge in juvenile court. Julia planned to be with him. She was proud that her efforts had helped to create the first court for children in the nation.

Julia's thoughts returned to her friends. Ellen was asking what Florence had been doing in New York. Florence tucked a stray hair back into place in her upswept hairdo. She began talking about her job as general secretary of the National Consumers League. The league studied working conditions in factories and other places where consumer goods such as clothing were made. It found out whether conditions were safe or not. If conditions were unsafe, the league told consumers not to buy goods from those places.

Florence also talked about the many speeches she was making about wages for working people. Some employers paid unfairly low wages. Poor people, desperate for money, were too often willing to work for such wages.

In the early 1900s, parents and children in the poorer areas of big cities worked together in their homes to earn money.

Florence wanted to get minimum wage laws passed. That way, workers would be sure to be paid fairly.

As the women talked, the fire burned low. Finally the grandfather clock struck two. Jane turned out the lights in the parlor as the tired women headed up the stairs. They could still get a few hours of sleep before morning. And they certainly needed the rest. It had been a busy day!

*The Jane Addams Hull-House Museum opened in 1967. Hull-House
has been restored to appear as it did when Jane Addams lived there.*

In my opinion, none of the national historical landmarks better signifies the achievements of the past while pointing the way to a brighter future for our cities than does Hull-House.

—Dr. Murray H. Nelligan of the National Park Service

Afterword

For many years after 1908, Hull-House continued to serve its community, changing and adapting as the city around it changed. Hull-House became a model for settlement houses around the nation.

Jane Addams's influence grew over time. She became a well-known member of several U.S. and international organizations working for social reform. She spoke out for women's right to vote, for racial equality, and for children's rights. She was a strong pacifist—a believer in nonviolent ways of settling conflicts. In 1931 Jane Addams became the first woman from the United States to be awarded the Nobel Peace Prize.

When Jane Addams died in 1935, residents, neighbors, and friends were deeply saddened. Louise deKoven Bowen took over running Hull-House. Most Hull-House programs continued.

Thanks to Julia Lathrop *(above left)*, Chicago officials created the first juvenile court in the world in 1899. She also served as the first chief of the Federal Children's Bureau, created in 1912. Jane Addams *(above, top photo)* served as president of the Women's International League for Peace and Freedom from 1915 to 1929. She won the Nobel Peace Prize in 1931. Dr. Alice Hamilton *(above right)* became the director of the Illinois Commission on Occupational Diseases. Her work led to the state's first worker's compensation law and other protections for workers in hazardous fields, such as the smelting of lead. Florence Kelley *(above, bottom photo)* was the general secretary of the National Consumers League for over thirty years. She also became vice president of the National American Woman Suffrage Association.

By 1958, however, the people who were coming to Hull-House were no longer only from the Nineteenth Ward. Many visitors lived in different parts of the huge city of Chicago. They had to travel a long way to get to Hull-House. Fewer and fewer people came.

In 1961 the city decided to tear down the Hull-House buildings. The land was needed for new buildings for the University of Illinois. Many people protested, but the plan went ahead anyway. Two buildings were left standing: the original Hull Mansion and the Residents' Dining Hall. In 1967 these two buildings became a museum—the Jane Addams Hull-House Museum—owned by the University of Illinois. The site also became a Chicago Landmark and a National Historic Landmark.

Around the museum, the Hull-House neighborhood has changed. Instead of tenement apartment houses, sky-scrapers loom nearby. Cars race down Halsted Street where horse-drawn carriages once rumbled.

In the Hull-House Museum, original furniture and signs help to tell the story of the most well-known U.S. settlement house.

Information about Hull-House's history surrounds the fireplace where Jane Addams and her friends discussed how to realize their dream of better conditions for American families.

But the Hull Mansion and the Residents' Dining Hall look much the same. Original furnishings, photographs, and paintings help to make them look just the way they did in 1889.

The Jane Addams Hull House Association continues to offer help to people all around Chicago. One of the programs of this agency is called Neighbor to Neighbor. The program helps to find foster homes for children who need foster care. These foster homes care for children in the same family and in their own community.

The Jane Addams Hull House Association helps to keep the spirit of Hull-House alive. That spirit also continues in a new kind of career—social work—that came from the work done at Hull-House. The social workers in the United States help to make cleaner cities, safer working conditions, and healthier families. Hull-House itself still receives guests, welcoming thousands of visitors from around the world each year.

Glossary

babushka: A woman's scarf worn on the head and tied under the chin

crèche: A nursery for very young children

immigrant: A person who leaves one country to live in another

settlement house: A community center in a poor, crowded neighborhood

sweatshop: A place where people work amid noise, dirt, and danger, often for pennies per day

tenement house: A three- or four-story apartment house. The lower floor was used as a stable and outhouse. The upper rooms contained cramped living quarters for several families.

Pronunciation Guide

babushka	bah-BOOSH-kah
crèche	KREHSH or KRAYSH
gymnasium	jihm-NAY-zee-uhm
Halsted	HAHL-stehd
suffrage	SUHF-rihj

Further Reading

Currie, Stephen. *We Have Marched Together: The Working Children's Crusade.* Minneapolis: Lerner Publications Company, 1997.

Harvey, Bonnie Carman. *Jane Addams: Nobel Prize Winner and Founder of Hull House.* Berkeley Heights, NJ: Enslow, 1999.

Kent, Deborah. *Jane Addams and Hull-House.* Chicago: Children's Press, 1992.

McPherson, Stephanie Sammartino. *Peace and Bread: The Story of Jane Addams.* Minneapolis: Carolrhoda Books, Inc., 1993.

Simon, Charnan. *Jane Addams: Pioneer Social Worker.* New York: Children's Press, 1997.

Touring Information

The Jane Addams Hull-House Museum is available for touring on weekdays from 10 A.M. to 4 P.M. and on Sundays from noon to 5 P.M. Admission is free.

Write to:
Jane Addams Hull-House Museum
The University of Illinois at Chicago
800 South Halsted Street
Chicago, IL 60607-7017

Or call:
(312) 413-5353

To learn more about Hull-House, visit these websites:
Hull House Association: <http://www.hullhouse.org>
Jane Addams Hull-House Museum:
<http://www.uic.edu/jaddams/hull/hull_house.html>

Index

About the Author

Laura B. Edge received her bachelor's degree in education from the University of Texas and went on to study educational concepts and philosophies at the American Institute of Foreign Study. She has worked as a teacher, computer programmer, and computer trainer. She is a member of the Society of Children's Book Writers and Illustrators and the Houston Writers League. She lives in Kingwood, Texas, with her husband and two children.

Acknowledgments

For quoted material: p. 5, Jane Addams, "Hull-House Women's Club Anthem," as reprinted in Mary Lynn McCree Bryan and Allen F. Davis, editors, *One Hundred Years at Hull-House* (Bloomington: Indiana University Press, 1990); p. 13, James Weber Linn, *Jane Addams: A Biography*, 113 (New York: D. Appleton-Century Company Incorporated, 1935); p. 23, Ibid., 132; p. 31, Bryan and Davis, *One Hundred Years at Hull-House*, 129 (a reprint of part of *And Crown Thy Good*, Philip Davis, pp. 85-93); p. 39, Hilda Satt Polacheck, *I Came a Stranger: The Story of a Hull-House Girl* (Urbana: University of Illinois Press, 1989), 91; p. 49, Jane Addams, *My Friend Julia Lathrop*, 74 (New York: The Macmillan Company, 1935); p. 57, Chicago Public Library website <http://cpl.lib.uic.edu/ 004chicago/timeline/hullhouse.html>.

For photos and artwork: Culver Pictures, pp. 1, 22, 29, 55; Chicago Historical Society, p. 4; Library of Congress, p. 6; Brown Brothers, p. 7; Jane Addams Memorial Collection, Special Collections, The University Library, The University of Illinois at Chicago, pp. 12, 14, 16, 19, 20, 25, 26, 28, 30, 32, 37, 38, 42, 46, 48, 51, 56, 59, 60; UPI/Corbis-Bettman, pp. 17, 35, 58 (bottom), 58 (right); Corbis-Bettman, p. 43; University of Illinois at Chicago, The University Library, Jane Addams Memorial Collection, Wallace Kirkland Papers, p. 44; UPI/Bettman, p. 53; © CORBIS, p. 58 (left), © Archive Photos p. 58 (top). All maps and artwork courtesy of Bryan Liedahl. Front cover courtesy of: Jane Addams Memorial Collection, Special Collections, The University Library, The University of Illinois at Chicago.